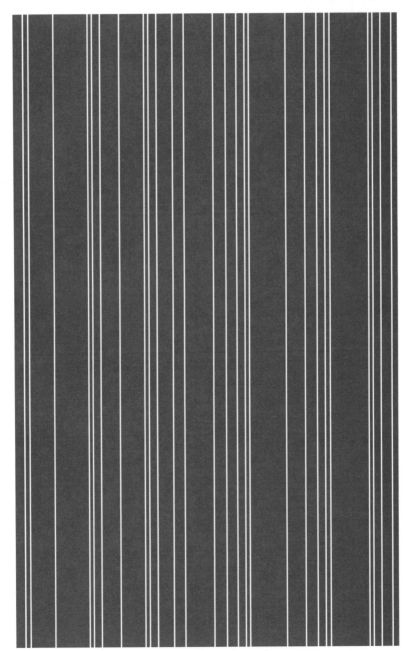

Nueva Salsa

RECIPES TO SPICE IT UP

BY RAFAEL PALOMINO AND ARLEN GARGAGLIANO
PHOTOGRAPHS BY MIKI DUISTERHOF

CHRONICLE BOOKS
SAN FRANCISCO

DEDICATION

I dedicate this book to my beautiful daughter, Amanda, whose love and laughter inspire me always. —Rafael Palomino

Dedico este libro a mi chef favorito, Rafael Palomino, who continues to dazzle me with his creativity—*y su sonrisa.* —Arlen Gargagliano

ACKNOWLEDGMENTS

Many thanks to: my writer, Arlen Gargagliano; my agent, Jane Dystel; my editor Bill Leblond, along with Amy Treadwell and the staff at Chronicle Books for all their support in making this project come to life; my Chronicle publicity manager, Michele Fuller; my Business partner, Moe Gad; my Managing staff: Angel Jurio, Alex Vanegas, and Juan Carlos Toro, and my chef de cuisine, Felix Perez; my kitchen-, wait-, and bar staff at Sonora and Vida; my publicists Steven Hall and Sam Firer at Steven Hall Public Relations; and especially—*with muchísimas* gracias y amor—to my family: my wife, Martha, my daughter, Amanda, my son, Rafael, my parents, Rafael and Graciela, my brother, Martin, and my sister, Gloria.

Library of Congress Cataloging-in-Publication Data available.

ISBN 0-8118-3697-5

Manufactured in China.

Prop styling by Philippa Braithwaite
Food styling by Alison Attenborough
Designed by Feel Good Anyway
Typesetting by Bill Morrison and Matt Eller
The photographer wishes to thank Steven Boljonis and Kathleen Stone

Distributed in Canada by Raincoast Books
9050 Shaughnessy Street
Vancouver, British Columbia V6P 6E5

10 9 8 7 6 5 4 3 2 1

CHRONICLE BOOKS LLC
85 Second Street
San Francisco, California 94105

www.chroniclebooks.com

Contents

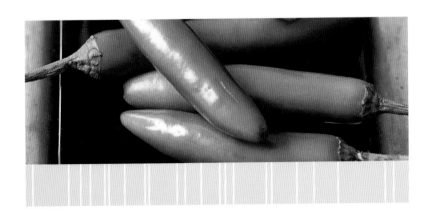

Introduction

Salsa— the word dances deliciously on your tongue. Whether music or food, salsa is vibrant. Salsa, the music, is an energy-inducing magic that lures even the most reluctant dancer to his or her feet. Salsa, the food, is the ultimate marriage of flavors and textures. Salsas add a foreground of exploding color and taste, complementing your favorite dish. They remind us of sunny days and sultry nights; they turn a celebration into a fiesta.

The Spanish word *salsa* means "sauce" in English. But salsa is *mucho más* (much more) than sauce. It's a rainbow of flavors. It's clean, it's fresh, and it's exciting. Sometimes loud with hot serranos, other times subtle and smoky with chipotle, salsa can also be soft and smooth when made with avocado, sweet when made with mango and papaya, or deeply flavored when made with *aguardiente* (Colombian brandy) and blackberries. Salsas can be made with fresh or cooked ingredients. In sauces there is a melding of flavors, while in salsas, each of the ingredients is *destacado*, or "outstanding"; each maintains its individual integrity.

Salsas are exciting and sexy; they should appeal to both your mind and palate. Creating a salsa is like composing a floral bouquet: The balance of color (both pale and bright) and texture (both soft and crunchy) is key. The basic rule for creating salsas is to use the freshest ingredients possible, then add vinegar and citrus juices to enhance the flavors.

Salsas are also like bouquets in that they are delicate. Fruit salsas are especially fragile and should be served shortly after preparing. Most salsas should sit for about 20 minutes at room temperature before serving so that the flavors marry. Refrigerated salsas should be brought to room temperature prior to serving. If you are making a salsa ahead of time, those using cooked ingredients are the best choice.

Salsa symbolizes how significantly food trends have evolved in the past fifteen years. In that time, salsa has leapt into the limelight. In 1991, U.S. sales of salsa beat those of ketchup by $40 million . In addition, the food industry has started doing what we've been doing in Latin America for hundreds of years: using spices—instead of fats—as flavor enhancers. *Por fin*, finally, the U.S. market is awakening!

This awakening is partly due to the many immigrant groups that have come—and continue to come—to the United States, as a walk through any supermarket will show. In addition to the abundance of Latino products—from fresh vegetables and seasonings to tortillas— there are chutneys from India, kimchees from Korea, jerk sauces from Jamaica, and tabboulehs from the Middle East—just to mention a few.

Furthermore, it's not just changes in palate that have boosted the popularity of salsas; it's also an increased awareness of what constitutes healthful cooking and eating. Salsas are usually very low in fat. Their basic ingredients—vegetables, chiles, fruits, beans, and grains—are clean and fresh. Their flavoring comes from vinegars, fresh herbs, and spices that add magic, not fat.

Salsa is elegant not only because it adds that special *toque* (touch) to so many dishes, but also because it is usually quite simple to prepare. The ingredients are not numerous, and preparation time is minimal. This means that whether you are struggling with that end-of-the-day pre-dinner craziness or mixing cocktails for a group of guests, you can take a few minutes and prepare something that will add *chispa* (spark) to whatever it is you're serving.

Salsas have always been an important part of my life. As a *muchacho* in Colombia, I was always armed with my spoon as my mother and *abuelita* (grandmother) prepared their *salsitas*, ranging from *salsa de ají picante* (spicy pepper salsa) to *salsas de frutas* (fruit salsas). I always loved the depth of flavor that salsas added to everything.

Thinking back now, I see that it was a trip to Mexico that led me into the world of salsa. My parents took us to Ixtapa, a beautiful village on the Pacific coast of Mexico. We dined every afternoon on a variety of local fare that was always enhanced by an accompanying salsa. We feasted on Pacific lobster, grilled over wood or boiled in seawater and scooped into freshly made tortillas, then topped with fresh cilantro and guacamole. We devoured grilled *pargo* (red snapper) with *pepián*, a rich Mexican classic sauce (found—with slight variations—in several parts of Mexico) of serrano chiles, cilantro, light cream, and pumpkin seeds. And we delighted in the many shrimp dishes, topped with salsas of chiles, cilantro, and tomatillos. As different as the salsas were from one another, they shared two common traits: They were fresh and *sabroso* (tasty), and they added *un toque muy especial*, a special touch, to the principal dish.

Later, when my family moved to New York and I got an after-school job working in Larry Forgione's River Café, my culinary horizons were broadened. (That's when my dream of becoming an engineer of cities was transformed into becoming an engineer of flavors!) Prepared with my copy of Louis Saulnier's classic *Le Répertoire de la Cuisine*, I began to develop a more in-depth knowledge of classic French cuisine. I learned about adding depth to sauce bases like wine, tomato, and chicken stock, and became familiar with sauces from aïoli to *zingara*.

These experiences helped to build the foundation of my flavor-combining skills, and I was hungry to learn more. When I was nineteen years old, I spent an incredible year in southern France, under the tutelage of French chef Michel Guérard. There I put into practice what I had begun to learn at the River Café: the fine art of blending herbs and spices. After my year abroad, I worked with chefs in New York—like Jonathan Waxman at Jams—from the school of New American cooking. They focused on using the freshest ingredients available. Now, in Vida, my New York City restaurant, and Sonora, my Port Chester, New York, restaurant, as well as in the recipes in my cookbooks *Bistro Latino* and *Viva la Vida*, I continue to practice the philosophy of healthful—and fun—cooking and eating.

I draw on all my experiences as I continue to increase my repertoire of salsas. In my restaurant kitchens we create salsas (as well as all the dishes on the menu) from a myriad of ingredients. Influences come from my Colombian roots, from my experiences in France and in New York, and from my coworkers. My Sonora restaurant partner, Moe Gad, has opened up a whole new world of flavors to me. A native of Egypt, Moe is well versed in the nuances of Middle Eastern cuisine. My kitchen staff, primarily from Mexico, also brings knowledge of foods from their homeland. *La parte más interesante*, the most interesting part, comes when we start blending things together—like Mexican chayote and Greek feta cheese, Korean kimchee and Caribbean mango—to deliver dazzling and delicious results. That's what this book is about: the fun and excitement of breaking the food barriers. I invite you to delight in these creations and to try to build your own! I'm sure you'll soon agree: Salsas are sublime.

Ingredient Glossary

During your travels to the local *supermercado*, you may have seen a lot of the ingredients used in these salsas, but you may not have been quite sure how to use them. This small glossary will give you the pronunciation for and a brief description of some the ingredients needed for salsas. Please note that some fruit and vegetable names in Spanish vary depending on the region.

AGUARDIENTE (*ah-guahr-DYEN-tay*), Colombia's national liquor, is an anise-flavored brandy made from sugarcane syrup. Aguardiente can usually be found in large liquor stores. If you can't find it, the Greek liquor ouzo is an acceptable substitute.

AJÍ AMARILLO (*ah-HEE ah-mah-REE-yo*) is a hot yellow chile used throughout Peru in many of its national dishes. Ají amarillo can be found in dried, ground, or paste form in Latin American markets or through mail order.

ANCHO (*AHN-cho*) **CHILES** are dried ripened poblano chiles. About 3 to 5 inches long and 2 to 4 inches wide, they have a rich mahogany color and a wrinkled skin. These chiles are relatively mild and slightly sweet. They're an essential ingredient in Mexican mole sauces.

CACHAÇA (*kah-CHA-hsa*), Brazil's national liquor and the main ingredient in the famous Brazilian cocktail *caipirinha*, is rum made from sugarcane. If cachaça is unavailable, light rum can be used as a substitute.

CHAYOTES (*chi-OH-tays*), which look like pear-shaped pale green gourds, were a principal food of the Aztecs and Mayas.

They're quite mild in flavor and can be used raw in salsas and salads, or baked like acorn squash. Chayotes are now grown in the United States and found in many large supermarkets.

CHIPOTLES (*chee-POHT-lays*) are ripened and smoked jalapeño chiles. These fiery hot Mexican chiles enhance many dishes with their fabulous smoky flavor. Chipotles are most often found in cans (chipotles en adobo) in supermarkets and Latino markets, preserved in a vinegar-and-tomato sauce.

CHORIZO (*chor-EE-soh*) is a pork sausage used in many Latin American dishes. Colombian chorizo, my personal favorite, can be found in Latin American markets either fresh or dried. If you can't find Colombian chorizo, the fresh Mexican chorizo is an acceptable—but slightly spicier—equivalent. Spanish chorizos are dry sausages.

GUAVAS (*GWAH-vas*) are a sweet tropical fruit now grown in parts of the United States. There are many varieties, but typically they are oval shaped and about the size of a small apple. Guava juice, jelly, paste, and marmalade are available in large supermarkets.

JALAPEÑOS (*hah-lah-PAYN-yos*) are probably the most commonly available fresh green chiles. Named after Jalapa, the capital of Veracruz, Mexico, they're small (2 to 3 inches long) and usually quite *picante*, or "hot." Fresh jalapeños have a smooth dark green skin and white seeds. They can be found in most large supermarkets.

PANELA (*pah-NAY-lah*), also known as **PILONCILLO** (*pee-lon-SEE-yoh*), is hardened brown cane sugar sold in loaves and cones throughout Latin America. It's the consistency of very hard dark brown sugar and can be easily grated. Panela can be found in Latino markets and through mail order. Dark or light brown sugar can be used as a substitute.

PLANTAINS, or **PLÁTANOS** (*PLAH-tah-nos*) have long been an important ingredient in Latin American cooking. These cooking bananas can be eaten at all stages of ripeness, from unripe green to yellow to fully ripe, or black. Plátanos look like overgrown bananas and can now be found in most large supermarkets. To sauté ripe plantains, dice them and sauté in 1 teaspoon canola oil over medium heat until they start to caramelize (about 5 to 7 minutes). To roast, preheat the oven to 450°F. Coat a baking sheet with canola oil or nonstick spray. Cut each plantain on the diagonal into ½-inch-thick slices. Brush the tops of the plantains with oil (or nonstick spray). Bake, turning occasionally, for about 12 minutes or until the plantains are golden brown and tender.

POBLANOS (*poh-BLAH-nos*) are dark green (sometimes almost black) fresh chiles with a rich flavor. While some poblanos are mild, others are quite hot. They're about 4 inches long and 2 ½ to 3 inches wide. Now grown in the United States, they are available in large supermarkets.

QUINOA (*KEY-noh-ah*), a grain now found in most supermarkets and natural foods stores, was a staple of the Incas. Similar in appearance to couscous, it is a tiny ivory-colored bead-shaped grain with a delicate, nutty flavor. Quinoa is considered a complete protein because it contains all eight essential amino acids.

ROCOTO (*roh-COH-toh*) is a hot red chile grown in Peru and other parts of South America. It can be found in paste form in Latin American markets.

SERRANOS (*say-RRAH-nos*) are small, slightly pointed fresh chiles with a hot, savory flavor. These chiles, whose green skin turns red when it ripens, are used in both fresh and cooked forms in a variety of salsas. They can be found in large supermarkets and Latino markets.

TOMATILLOS (*toh-mah-TEE-yos*), also called Mexican green tomatoes, belong to the same nightshade family as the tomato. They look like little green tomatoes, but they have a papery husk. To use, peel off the husk and rinse the fruit. Tomatillos can ripen to a yellow color, but they are usually used when firm and green. Found in large supermarkets and Latino markets, this fruit can be used in both raw and cooked form.

Fruit Salsas

(*Salsas de Frutas*)

A walk through a fruit market is invigorating. Bright mountains of fruit, like spring-green limes or fiery-sunset oranges, are inspirational. From Siete de Agosto, my childhood *mercado* in Bogotá, to the local fruit and vegetable markets I frequent near my New York restaurants and home, *la belleza es igual*, the beauty of fresh fruit is the same.

Fresh-fruit salsas capture vibrant color and intricate flavors. *Lo importante*, the important thing, is to buy excellent-quality fruit. Combine your *salsas de frutas* with your favorite fish, meat, and tortilla chips. You'll be inspired to try your own combinations.

Grapefruit, Cucumber, and Mint Salsa

I'm always looking for new ways to dress up a salad. This easy, light Middle Eastern–inspired salsa works well atop fresh arugula or any other greens.

MAKES ABOUT 3 CUPS

Stripped zest of ¼ orange

3 pink grapefruits, peeled, seeded, and cut into segments (page 118)

3 cucumbers, seeded and diced

Juice of 1 orange

10 fresh mint leaves, stacked, rolled, and cut into fine shreds

• In a small saucepan of boiling water, blanch the orange zest for 10 seconds. Drain immediately and let cool to room temperature.

•• In a large bowl, combine the grapefruits and cucumbers. Stir in the orange juice and drained zest. Let sit for about 20 minutes, then stir in the mint leaves and serve. Or, cover and refrigerate for up to 3 days. Return to room temperature and stir in the mint leaves just before serving.

Fig and Roasted Yellow Tomato Salsa

This exotic salsa is guaranteed to seduce even a non-fig-lover! The ginger-kissed reduced caipirinha enhances all the flavors in this mélange. Friends raved when I served this salsa on grilled tuna.

MAKES ABOUT 2 CUPS

1 recipe caipirinha (page 119)

1 tablespoon minced fresh ginger

10 medium-size fresh figs, stemmed and coarsely chopped (about 2 cups)

1 roasted yellow tomato (page 117), coarsely chopped

$\frac{1}{4}$ cup canola oil

2 tablespoons white balsamic vinegar

• In a small saucepan, cook the caipirinha and ginger over medium-high heat until the liquid is reduced by half. Remove from heat.

•• Meanwhile, in a large bowl, combine the figs, tomato, oil, and vinegar. Stir well, using your hand or a wooden spoon. Add the caipirinha mixture and stir to blend. Let sit for about 20 minutes before serving. Or, cover and refrigerate for up to 1 day. Return to room temperature before serving.

Mango, Cucumber, and Cumin Salsa

This cumin-sprinkled salsa is ideally served on a piece of grilled fish or a tuna burger. The soft mango contrasts nicely with the crisp cucumber.

MAKES ABOUT 3 CUPS

2 mangos, peeled, cut from the pit, and cut into $1/4$-inch dice

1 cucumber, seeded and finely diced

$1/4$ cup mango nectar

2 tablespoons olive oil

5 tablespoons white balsamic vinegar

$1/4$ teaspoon ground cumin, or to taste

2 tablespoons chopped fresh chives

• In a large bowl, combine the mangos, cucumber, and mango nectar. Stir well, using your hand or a wooden spoon. Stir in all the remaining ingredients except the chives. Let sit for about 20 minutes, then stir in the chives and serve. Or, cover and refrigerate for up to 2 days. Return to room temperature and stir in the chives just before serving.

Raspberry and Port-Rioja Salsa

This salsa will make you swoon. I love its velvet deep color and mixed fruity and winey flavor. Though you may find other ways to serve this salsa, I like it on soft-shell crabs or red snapper.

MAKES ABOUT 3 CUPS

1/3 cup port wine

1/3 cup red Rioja wine

Grated zest of 1/2 orange

3 whole cloves

1 teaspoon sugar

Pinch of ground cinnamon

2 cups fresh raspberries

1 mango, peeled, cut from the pit, and cut into 1/4-inch dice

Juice of 1/2 lime

1/4 cup crème de cassis liqueur

2 teaspoons thinly sliced fresh mint leaves

• In a small saucepan, combine the port, Rioja, orange zest, cloves, and sugar. Stir over medium heat. Add the cinnamon and simmer for 10 to 15 minutes, until reduced by half. Remove from heat and let cool to room temperature. Remove the cloves.

• • In a medium bowl, combine the raspberries and mango. Add the wine mixture, lime juice, and crème de cassis. Let sit for about 20 minutes, then stir in the mint and serve.

Pear, Merlot, and Dill Salsa

Ever since I was a little boy in Colombia, my family has enjoyed pork prepared in many different ways, ranging from our traditional Christmas *lechón*, roast suckling pig, to *chicharrones*, pork cracklings. In fact, thanks to early colonists from Portugal and Spain, pork is common throughout Latin America. Today I like to use pork as a tasty backdrop for a variety of fruit-based salsas. Here's one that incorporates the tropical *toque*, or touch, of mango with pear, Merlot, and dill.

MAKES ABOUT 2½ CUPS

3 Bartlett pears, peeled, cored, and cut into ¼-inch dice

½ bottle Merlot wine

2 tablespoons sugar

¼ mango, peeled, cut from the pit, and cut into ¼-inch dice

2 tablespoons chopped fresh dill

• In a medium saucepan, combine the pears, Merlot, and sugar. Stir to mix. Bring to a boil over high heat, reduce heat to low, and simmer for 7 to 10 minutes, or until crisp-tender. Remove from heat and pour into a bowl. Let cool to room temperature. Stir in the mango. Let sit for about 20 minutes, then stir in the dill and serve. Or, cover and refrigerate for up to 2 days. Return to room temperature and stir in the dill just before serving.

Peach and Chayote Salsa

I learned about the wonders of chayote from my Mexican coworkers in New York City restaurants. This gourdlike fruit is quite versatile because its natural flavor is relatively mild. Here, it works well with peaches, orange juice, and ají in a refreshing salsa to serve on grilled fish or a salad.

MAKES ABOUT 7 CUPS

2 chayotes, peeled

1 cup fresh orange juice

4 peaches, peeled, pitted, and diced

1 cucumber, peeled, seeded, and diced

2 tablespoons white balsamic vinegar

⅓ cup olive oil

2 teaspoons ají amarillo

• Cook the chayotes in simmering water for 25 minutes, or until soft. Drain and let cool to room temperature. Seed and dice.

• • Meanwhile, bring the orange juice to a simmer in a small saucepan and cook for 5 to 7 minutes until reduced by half. Remove from heat and let cool to room temperature.

• • • In a large bowl, combine the chayotes, peaches, and cucumber. Add the orange juice, vinegar, oil, and ají. Stir to blend. Let sit for about 20 minutes before serving. Or, cover and refrigerate for up to 2 days. Return to room temperature before serving.

Watermelon, Tequila, and Pineapple Salsa

Even on the dreariest of wintry New York days, fruit salsas can bring a smile to my face. This tequila-kissed salsa is a great match for snapper or swordfish. Look for seedless watermelon; it's slightly sweeter than the variety with seeds—and it's a lot easier to work with. Make sure you refrigerate this salsa for at least 1 hour before serving.

MAKES ABOUT 4 CUPS

3 cups diced seeded watermelon

$1/2$ pineapple, peeled, cored, and diced (about 2 cups)

$1/3$ cup tequila

1 roasted poblano chile (page 117), peeled, seeded, and diced

3 tablespoons chopped fresh cilantro

Juice of 1 orange

Juice of 1 lime

1 teaspoon rocoto paste or chipotle purée (page 120)

1 teaspoon rice vinegar

Kosher salt and freshly ground pepper to taste

• In a large bowl, combine the watermelon, pineapple, and tequila. Stir to blend. Stir in all the remaining ingredients. Cover and refrigerate for at least 1 hour before serving. Or, cover and refrigerate for up to 1 day.

Pear and Lentil Salsa

This gorgeous combination of flavors and textures could be a meal by itself! Black beluga lentils, a hybrid of the prized French Le Puy green lentils , keep their shape when cooked and turn a deep blackish green. Beluga lentils have a soft, creamy interior and offer a welcome color and flavor contrast to pear and mango. This salsa is ideal served over grilled cod.

MAKES ABOUT 4 CUPS

4 Bartlett or Anjou pears, peeled, cored, and finely diced

$1/2$ cup unsweetened grated coconut

$3/4$ cup drained cooked black beluga or green lentils

1 cup shredded or finely julienned mango

$1/4$ cup white balsamic vinegar

$1/4$ cup olive oil

2 teaspoons ají amarillo

1 tablespoon chopped fresh chives

• In a large bowl, combine the pears, coconut, and lentils. Stir in all the remaining ingredients except the chives. Let sit for about 20 minutes, then stir in the chives and serve. Or, cover and refrigerate for up to 2 days. Return to room temperature and stir in the chives just before serving.

Strawberry, Kiwi, and Caipirinha Salsa

The magical flavors of the Brazilian caiprinha inspire me not only to dance the samba and learn Portuguese but also to create luscious fruit combinations. A touch of grated coconut adds a nice color and flavor contrast to this delicate salsa. A great match with soft-shell crabs, it should be made as close to serving time as possible.

MAKES ABOUT 3 CUPS

6 kiwis, peeled and diced (about 2 cups)

1½ cups fresh strawberries, hulled and diced

¾ cup fresh raspberries

¼ cup caipirinha (page 119)

2 teaspoons white balsamic vinegar

⅓ cup sweetened grated coconut

• In a large bowl, combine the kiwis, strawberries, and raspberries. Stir in all the remaining ingredients. Serve immediately

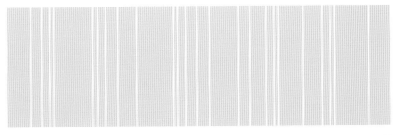

Tropical Salsas

(*Salsas Tropicales*)

The scent of passion fruit is intoxicating. The flavors of papaya, mango, pineapple, and guava are deep and fragrant. Salsas made with tropical fruits send us to places where we are kissed by breezes and embraced by sunshine.

Salsas tropicales are festive splashes of color that can adorn everything from chips to fish. Just as you enjoy wading in clear, warm Caribbean waters, you'll relish the *ricos sabores*, or delicious flavors, of these salsas.

Papaya and Poblano Chile Salsa

When my wife was pregnant, first with Amanda and then with Rafael, she was told that papaya would help alleviate her morning sickness. Toward the end of both pregnancies, she was told that eating spicy food would help bring on labor. But of course you don't have to be expecting to enjoy this *rica* (delicious) salsa! Though poblano chiles can be quite *picante* (hot), the papaya softens the blow and adds its own delicate flavor. This spicy salsa marries well with mahimahi or grilled chicken.

MAKES ABOUT 2 CUPS

1/2 papaya, peeled, seeded, and finely diced

1 roasted poblano chile (page 117), peeled, seeded, and finely diced

1/4 cup diced red onion

Juice of 1 orange

Juice of 1 lime

1/2 cup chopped fresh cilantro

2 teaspoons rocoto paste or chipotle purée (page 120), or to taste

• In a large bowl, combine the papaya, chile, onion, and orange and lime juices. Stir well, using your hand or a wooden spoon. Let marinate for at least 5 minutes but no longer than 15 minutes. Stir in the cilantro and rocoto paste or chipotle purée. Serve immediately.

Mango, Plantain, and Coconut Salsa

This Colombia-inspired salsa blends beautifully with a salmon *tiradito* (thin slices of fresh salmon) or with any fish, such as grilled snapper or Chilean sea bass. My customers also enjoy this tropical fruit salsa served on top of steaming white rice.

MAKES ABOUT 2¼ CUPS

1 mango, peeled, cut from the pit, and finely diced

1 very ripe (black) plantain, diced

2 teaspoons unsweetened grated coconut

¼ cup white balsamic vinegar

Juice of ½ lime

Pinch of grated lime zest

2 tablespoons chopped fresh chives

• In a medium bowl, combine the mango, plantain, and coconut. Stir in all the remaining ingredients except the chives. Let sit for about 20 minutes, then stir in the chives and serve. Or, cover and refrigerate for up to 3 days. Return to room temperature and stir in the chives just before serving.

Passion Fruit and Citrus Salsa

I love dazzling my customers with this stunning salsa served on mahi mahi. The flavors and colors of the passion fruit and citrus offer the perfect foreground for the mild fish. To cut the citrus fruit into segments, see page 118.

MAKES ABOUT 4 CUPS

$\frac{1}{2}$ red onion, thinly sliced

$\frac{7}{8}$ cup (7 ounces) passion fruit pulp

2 tablespoons honey

$\frac{1}{2}$ cup water

3 grapefruits, peeled and cut into segments (page 118)

4 oranges, peeled and cut into segments (page 118)

1 lime, peeled and cut into segments (page 118)

1 tablespoon $\frac{1}{4}$-inch diagonally cut fresh chives

• Blanch the onion by placing in a strainer and submerging it in boiling water for about 5 minutes, or until softened. Drain and let cool.

• • In the same saucepan, combine the passion fruit pulp, honey, and water. Bring to a boil, reduce heat to a simmer, and cook for about 10 minutes, until reduced by half. Remove from heat and let cool to room temperature.

• • • In a large bowl, combine the grapefruit, orange, and lime segments. Add the blanched onion and stir. Pour off about half the liquid. Stir in the cooled passion fruit mixture. Stir in the chives and serve. Or, cover and refrigerate for up to 3 days. Return to room temperature and stir in the chives just before serving.

Pineapple, Coconut, and Ginger Salsa

If I close my eyes when I taste this salsa, I can see the gorgeous beaches of Brazil. Men with carts of fresh coconuts travel the beaches there, ready to hack open their luscious fruits so that beachgoers can enjoy fresh, cooling coconut water, and then the meat of the fruit. In São Paulo, where there is the largest population of Japanese people outside of Japan, the tropical fruit flavors are blended with Japanese cuisine. (For example, there you can find California rolls made with fresh mango.) This pineapple, coconut, and ginger salsa is delicious on steamed fish such as snapper, salmon, and halibut, as well as on steaming white rice.

MAKES ABOUT 2½ CUPS

½ pineapple, peeled, cored, and cut into ¼-inch dice

1-inch piece fresh ginger, grated

1 teaspoon cream of coconut

¼ cup coconut milk

Juice of ½ lime

5 fresh mint leaves, stacked, rolled, and cut into fine shreds

• In a medium glass or ceramic bowl, combine the pineapple, ginger, cream of coconut, and coconut milk. Stir to blend. Stir in the lime juice. Let sit for about 20 minutes, then stir in the mint and serve. Or, cover and refrigerate for up to 3 days. Return to room temperature and stir in the mint just before serving.

Pineapple and Caipirinha Salsa

This salsa is definitely for the 21-and-over crowd. Caipirinha, the national lime and cachaça (Brazilian rum) cocktail of Brazil, adds a samba-inspiring taste to any dish. Recently, I shared this recipe with a friend who asked, "If you only use half a caipirinha, what do you do with the other half?" My reply was obvious. "You drink it, *por supuesto* (of course)!" Clean, fresh, and elegant, this salsa goes as well with salmon as it does with sea bass or any nice piece of fish.

MAKES ABOUT 1½ CUPS

½ pineapple, peeled, cored, and cut into ¼-inch dice
½ recipe caipirinha (page 119), strained
1 tablespoon finely shredded fresh mint leaves

• In a large bowl, combine the pineapple and caipirinha. Stir to blend. Let sit for about 20 minutes, then stir in the mint and serve. Or, cover and refrigerate for up to 3 days. Return to room temperature and stir in the mint just before serving.

Guava, Lime, and Ancho Chile Salsa

This richly flavored maroon-colored salsa is an excellent match with any game dish, such as squab, quail, duck—or even free-range chicken.

MAKES ABOUT 2½ CUPS

2 ancho chiles

1-pound bar guava paste, diced (paste is quite sticky, so use a wet knife to dice)

Juice of 2 limes

Kosher salt and freshly ground pepper to taste

• In a medium saucepan of boiling water, cook the chiles for about 8 minutes, or until softened. Drain and let cool to the touch. Dice.

•• In a medium bowl, combine the chiles and diced guava paste. Stir in the lime juice, salt, and pepper. Let sit for about 20 minutes before serving. Or, cover and refrigerate for up to 3 days. Return to room temperature before serving.

Grilled Pineapple and Lime Salsa

I discovered the flavors of grilled pineapple and lime at La Concha, a restaurant in the gorgeous Las Brisas resort in Acapulco, Mexico. Grilling the pineapple gives it a wonderful roasted, sweet flavor, which is beautifully balanced by the fresh lime and orange juices. This particular salsa is great served on mahi mahi, swordfish, or snapper.

MAKES ABOUT 2 CUPS

1 tablespoon olive oil, plus 1 teaspoon

$^1/_2$ large pineapple, peeled, cut into nine $^1/_4$-inch-thick slices, and cored

1 red bell pepper, seeded, deribbed, and finely diced

Juice of 1 orange

Juice of 1 lime

$^1/_4$ teaspoon grated lime zest

• Heat the 1 tablespoon oil in a large skillet over medium-high heat. Using tongs, transfer the pineapple slices to the pan in batches and sauté until browned on both sides, 3 to 5 minutes. Remove from heat and let cool to room temperature.

•• Cut the pineapple into $^1/_4$-inch dice. In a large bowl, combine the pineapple, bell pepper, orange juice, and lime juice. Stir in the lime zest. Let sit for about 20 minutes before serving. Or, cover and refrigerate for up to 3 days. Return to room temperature before serving.

Passion Fruit and Strawberry Salsa

This sweet, colorful salsa is a gorgeous and flavorful addition to grilled langostinos or jumbo shrimp.

MAKES ABOUT 3 CUPS

7/8 cup (7 ounces) passion fruit pulp

2 tablespoons honey

1 cup water

4 cups fresh strawberries, hulled and chopped

2 bunches mâche (field lettuce)

• In a small saucepan, combine the passion fruit pulp, honey, and water. Bring to a boil. Reduce heat and simmer for about 10 minutes, until reduced by half. Remove from heat and let cool to room temperature.

•• In a large bowl, combine the passion fruit mixture, strawberries, and mâche. Toss to mix. Serve immediately.

Chorizo and Plantain Salsa

There are certain taste combinations I swoon over; chorizo and sweet plantain is one of them. This salsa easily stands alone (I eat it by the spoonful), but works beautifully dolloped on top of a spinach salad.

1 very ripe (black) plantain, diced (about 1 cup)

1 roasted fresh Colombian, Mexican, or Spanish chorizo,
  cut into ¼-inch dice

Kernels cut from 2 ears roasted corn (page 117),
  or 1 cup roasted corn kernels (page 117)

3 plum tomatoes, seeded and diced (about 1 cup)

½ cup white balsamic vinegar

6 tablespoons canola oil

Kosher salt and freshly ground pepper to taste

1 tablespoon coarsely chopped fresh chives

• In a large bowl, combine the plantain, chorizo, and roasted corn. Stir well, using your hand or a wooden spoon. Stir in all the remaining ingredients except the chives. Let sit for about 20 minutes, then stir in the chives and serve. Or, cover and refrigerate for up to 3 days. Return to room temperature and stir in the chives just before serving.

Papaya, Chipotle, and Yogurt Salsa

Martha, my wife, loves salads and is always looking for new ways to dress them. This simple, smoky salsa adds a lot of spark to a bed of romaine lettuce.

1/2 papaya, peeled, seeded, and finely diced (about 2 cups)

1/4 cup plain yogurt

2 teaspoons chipotle purée (page 120) or rocoto paste

Juice of 1/2 lime

• In a large bowl, combine the papaya, yogurt, and chipotle purée or rocoto paste. Stir well, using your hand or a wooden spoon. Stir in the lime juice and serve. Or, cover and refrigerate for up to 2 days. Return to room temperature before serving.

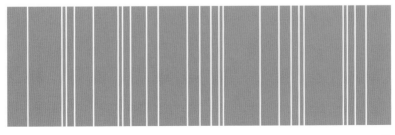

New Exotics

(Nuevas Exoticas)

Discovering a new flavor is like arriving in a foreign land for the first time: Your senses are heightened, everything is new and exciting, and you feel energized. Combining exotic tastes with more familiar ones is a way of testing the waters; you can dabble without diving in.

These salsas combine familiar Colombian ingredients with those from other parts of Latin America, as well as from Asia and the Middle East. Once you start to enjoy this fusion of flavors, you'll be inspired to continue.

Middle Eastern–Latino Eggplant Salsa

Eggplant was introduced to me not in my native Colombia, but in the States when I began to work for Larry Forgione at the River Café. After spending a year in France, I began to explore the wonders of this versatile and tasty vegetable. Most recently—and due in part to my partnership with an Egyptian—I've begun exploring new territory as far as my eggplant recipes are concerned. This recipe is a kind of Latino baba ghanoush, a Middle Eastern eggplant purée used as a spread or dip for pita bread. I have served this with sautéed jumbo shrimp, as well as a sauce for rigatoni or penne pasta.

MAKES ABOUT 2½ CUPS

5 roasted Japanese eggplants (page 117)

½ red onion, finely chopped

1 *each* roasted red and yellow bell pepper (page 117), peeled, seeded, and julienned

Pinch of ground cumin

½ cup olive oil

¼ cup white balsamic vinegar

Kosher salt and freshly ground pepper to taste

Handful of coarsely chopped fresh cilantro

• Slice the eggplants lengthwise and spoon out the flesh. Coarsely chop and put into a large bowl. Add the red onion and bell peppers. Stir in the cumin, oil, vinegar, salt, and pepper. Stir again. Let sit for about 20 minutes, then stir in the cilantro and serve. Or, cover and refrigerate for up to 3 days. Return to room temperature and stir in the cilantro just before serving.

Quinoa Tabbouleh Salsa

Meeting my Sonora partner, Moe Gad, who hails from Egypt and whose wife is Moroccan, not only signified the beginning of a great relationship, it also marked the beginning of my voyage into the world of Middle Eastern cooking. Moe gets just as excited as I do about combining elements of our native cuisines, so he was thrilled to try this variation of the traditional bulgur wheat, tomato, and parsley tabbouleh. According to Moe, this salsa is a great side dish. I like to serve it over a nice piece of grilled red snapper or a bed of fresh greens.

MAKES ABOUT 4 CUPS

1 bunch parsley, stemmed and coarsely chopped

1 red onion, finely chopped

4 plum tomatoes, diced

1/2 cup olive oil

1 very ripe (black) plantain, diced

1/2 cup soybean oil

1/2 cup cooked quinoa (page 116)

Juice of 1/2 lime

3 tablespoons white balsamic vinegar

Kosher salt and freshly ground pepper to taste

1 teaspoon minced fresh mint

• In a large bowl, combine the parsley, onion, and tomatoes. Add the olive oil and plantains, then stir in all the remaining ingredients except the mint. Let sit for about 20 minutes, then stir in the mint and serve. Or, cover and refrigerate for up to 3 days. Return to room temperature and stir in the mint just before serving.

Papaya, Lime, and Candied Ginger Salsa

The clean, tropical flavors of this beautiful Latino-Asian salsa make it a natural for snapper or ceviche. I also like to serve it with a sea bass *tiradito*: very thin slices of raw fish.

MAKES ABOUT 3 CUPS

1/2 papaya, peeled, seeded, and diced

2 limes, peeled and cut into segments (page 118),
  plus juice of 2 limes

2 oranges, peeled and cut into segments (page 118)

1/4 cup candied ginger (1 1/2 ounces), diced

Pinch *each* of salt and freshly ground pepper

• In a large bowl, combine all the ingredients and stir to blend. Let sit for about 20 minutes before serving. Or, cover and refrigerate for up to 3 days. Return to room temperature before serving.

Quinoa, Mango, and Cilantro Salsa

Though I only recently discovered the wonders of quinoa when I was in Peru, this grain was a staple of the ancient Incas hundreds of years ago. Today, Peruvians—and many other health-conscious people around the globe—have discovered, as I have, that quinoa can be happily combined with a variety of other foods. This salsa can be served on grilled fish or a salad of mixed greens.

MAKES ABOUT 3 CUPS

1 roasted red onion (page 117), cut into ¼-inch dice

2 ripe mangoes, peeled, cut from the pit, and cut into ¼-inch dice

1 cup cooked quinoa (page 116)

¼ cup white balsamic vinegar

1 cup mango nectar

Freshly ground pepper to taste

¼ cup coarsely chopped fresh cilantro

• In a large bowl, combine the onion, mangoes, quinoa, vinegar, and mango nectar. Stir well, using your hand or a wooden spoon. Stir in the pepper. Let sit for about 20 minutes, then stir in the cilantro and serve. Or, cover and refrigerate for up to 5 days. Return to room temperature and stir in the cilantro just before serving.

Japanese Cucumber and Papaya Salsa

What impresses me most about Japanese cuisine, aside from its fabulous flavors, is its presentation: Food is delicately displayed in a balance of color and form. Since arriving in New York, I've been constantly dazzled by the arrangement of Japanese food, which has definitely affected my own food presentation. In color, texture, and flavor, this salsa is simply *riquísimo*, or "delicious!" The mild-flavored Japanese cucumber, similar to an English (hothouse) cucumber, is long and green skinned, with edible seeds. The fresh, clean flavors of this salsa make it ideal to scoop up with chips, to spoon on top of a salad of mixed greens, or to serve on a piece of grilled fish such as snapper.

MAKES ABOUT 4 CUPS

1 Japanese or English (hothouse) cucumber, seeded and diced

1/2 papaya, peeled, seeded, and diced (about 2 cups)

1/3 cup diagonally sliced green onions (green parts only)

1/2 cup white balsamic vinegar

1/2 cup olive oil

2 teaspoons ají amarillo

Juice of 1/2 lime

• In a large bowl, combine the cucumber, papaya, and green onions. Stir to blend. Stir in all the remaining ingredients. Let sit for about 20 minutes before serving. Or, cover and refrigerate for up to 3 days. Return to room temperature before serving.

Kimchee and Mango Salsa

Kimchee is to Koreans as chimichurri is to Argentines: a necessary condiment. Though there are literally hundreds of kimchees (depending on both the region and the family of the makers), it's usually made with fermented cabbage and turnips. This Latino version is not as *picante* as its forefathers. The cabbage is blanched slightly, then sweetened with the addition of mango and pineapple. The results are a refreshing kind of coleslaw that's ideally served on a tuna burger, grilled fish, or a salad of mixed greens.

MAKES ABOUT 5 CUPS

1/2 cabbage, cored and thinly sliced

1 mango, peeled, cut from the pit, and julienned

1/2 cup white balsamic vinegar

1 cup mango nectar

1 cup diced fresh pineapple

Juice of 1 lime

Kosher salt and freshly ground pepper to taste

1 tablespoon minced fresh chives

• Cook the sliced cabbage in boiling water for 2 minutes, or until lightly softened. Drain and let cool to room temperature.

• • In a large bowl, combine the mango and vinegar. Stir in the mango nectar, pineapple, lime juice, salt, and pepper. Let sit for about 20 minutes, then stir in the chives and serve. Or, cover and refrigerate for up to 3 days. Return to room temperature and stir in the chives just before serving.

Nori and Papaya Salsa

Nori—paper-thin sheets of dried seaweed—is found in virtually every market in the New York area and in large supermarkets around the country. Originally from Japan, nori is traditionally used to wrap sushi or rice balls, but it can also be cut into thin strips (using a sharp knife or, as my coauthor prefers, poultry shears) and used as a garnish or seasoning. I buy *yakinori*, which is nori that has been slightly toasted. Here, I've combined the slightly sweet ocean flavor of nori with the tropical flavor of fresh papaya. The results are *fabuloso!* The contrast of textures, as well as that of the pale orange and rich black-purple colors, is just gorgeous. I like this salsa scooped on top of a mixed green salad or on tofu.

MAKES ABOUT 3 CUPS

3 sheets toasted nori, cut into 1/2-inch squares

1/2 papaya, peeled, seeded, and diced (about 2 cups)

Juice of 1 lime

1 cup mango nectar

2 tablespoons rice wine vinegar

Kosher salt and freshly ground pepper to taste

1 bunch chives, cut into 1/4-inch-long pieces

• Blanch the nori in boiling water for 10 seconds (it will wilt immediately). Drain and set aside to cool.

• • In a large glass or ceramic bowl, combine the papaya, lime juice, and mango nectar. Stir to blend. Add the vinegar, nori, salt, and pepper. Use your hands or a wooden spoon to gently toss. Let sit for about 20 minutes, then stir in the chives and serve. Or, cover and refrigerate for up to 1 day. Return to room temperature and stir in the chives just before serving.

Feta Cheese Salsa

Feta cheese adds a welcome rich and salty flavor to a variety of Greek and Middle Eastern dishes. In this salsa, the classic Greek cheese is beautifully balanced by olives, red onions, and chayote. Serve it on top of a spinach salad or any mixed green salad. It's also nice dolloped on grilled fish.

MAKES ABOUT 4½ CUPS

8 ounces feta cheese, crumbled or shredded

1 chayote, peeled, seeded, and diced

1 cup kalamata olives, pitted and coarsely chopped

¼ red onion, sliced and breaded

3 tablespoons white balsamic vinegar

3 tablespoons olive oil

Pinch of ground cloves

Kosher salt and freshly ground pepper to taste

• In a large bowl, combine the cheese, chayote, and olives. Stir in all the remaining ingredients. Let sit for about 20 minutes before serving. Or, cover and refrigerate for up to 3 days. Return to room temperature before serving.

Manchego Cheese and Kalamata Olive Salsa

Manchego cheese, so named because it was originally made only from the milk of the Manchego sheep that grazed the plains of La Mancha, Spain, is rich and mellow flavored. Serve this colorful Mediterranean salsa on top of freshly toasted French or Italian bread. Accompany with a group of friends, a nice bottle of red Rioja wine, and a roaring winter fire.

MAKES ABOUT 3 ½ CUPS

3/4 cup (6 ounces) finely diced manchego cheese

1 roasted red onion (page 117), sliced

1 cup kalamata olives, pitted and halved

1 red bell pepper, roasted, peeled, and julienned (page 117)

1 cup olive oil

1/2 cup white balsamic vinegar

1 tablespoon minced fresh thyme

Kosher salt and freshly ground pepper to taste

• In a large bowl, combine the cheese (making sure to separate the pieces as much as possible), onion slices, and olives. Stir to blend. Stir in all the remaining ingredients. Let sit for about 20 minutes before serving. Or, cover and refrigerate for up to 3 days. Return to room temperature before serving.

Avocado and Wasabi Salsa

Ever since I came to New York, I've been having a love affair with the culinary delights of Japan. I like to play around with the flavors of Latin American and Japanese cooking. Here, I've created a Japanese "guacamole." Unlike its traditional Mexican counterpart, it's sparked with ginger and wasabi (you may want to use more or less ginger and wasabi according to your personal taste). This salsa is excellent with any kind of chip.

MAKES ABOUT 3 CUPS

2 ripe Hass avocados, peeled, pitted and coarsely chopped

1 small red onion, diced

Juice of ¹/₂ lime

¹/₄ cup canola oil

1 tablespoon grated fresh ginger

2 teaspoons wasabi powder blended with water, or to taste

¹/₄ cup white balsamic vinegar

Kosher salt and freshly ground pepper to taste

1 teaspoon minced fresh cilantro

• In a large glass or ceramic bowl, combine the avocados, onion, and lime juice. Add all the remaining ingredients except the cilantro. Toss gently. Let sit for about 20 minutes, then stir in the cilantro and serve. Or, cover and refrigerate for up to 1 day. Return to room temperature and stir in the cilantro just before serving.

Tomato Salsas

(*Salsas de Tomates*)

Pomme d'amour ("love apple") was the name that the French gave the tomato after explorers discovered it in the New World. Though it may not really be an aphrodisiac, the tomato is luscious and sensuous. Red, green, yellow, or even purple in color, tomatoes are the ingredient perhaps most identified with salsa.

Today's *salsas de tomates* include a wealth of collaborating flavors, including other vegetables, herbs,and nuts. Whether roasted or fresh, this fruit's slightly sweet flavors are perfect in salsas that will complement many different foods.

Tomato, Avocado, and Cilantro Salsa (*Ají Rojo*)

Fans of all ages enjoy this great party salsa. Wes, my coauthor's nine-year-old son, forgoes the chips and asks for a dish of *ají rojo* and a spoon! I usually serve this with malanga, plantain, or yuca chips.

MAKES ABOUT 4½ CUPS

2 ripe Hass avocados, peeled, pitted, and cut into ¼-inch dice

1 red onion, finely diced

6 plum tomatoes, seeded and finely diced

2 cups tomato juice

½ cup white balsamic vinegar

2 teaspoons chipotle purée (page 120), or rocoto paste or to taste

Juice of ½ lime

Kosher salt and freshly ground pepper to taste

1 cup chopped fresh cilantro

• In a large bowl, combine the avocados, red onion, tomatoes, and tomato juice. Gently stir with a wooden spoon or your hand just until blended. Gently stir in the chipotle purée or rocoto paste, lime juice, salt, and pepper. Let sit for about 20 minutes, then stir in the cilantro and serve. Or, cover and refrigerate for up to 1 day. Return to room temperature and stir in the cilantro just before serving.

Sun-Dried Tomato Chimichurri

You couldn't visit the famous Argentine *parilladas*, or steak houses, without noticing the ubiquitous bottles of chimichurri, the thick herb sauce served with grilled meat. Chimichurri is traditionally made with parsley, oregano, olive oil, vinegar, and garlic. This is one of my chimichurri variations. The flavors of sun-dried tomatoes and white balsamic vinegar combine to make a simple dip for plantain chips, or a light garnish for grilled sirloin, salmon, or even roasted vegetables.

MAKES ABOUT 1½ CUPS

½ cup dry-packed sun-dried tomatoes,
  soaked in hot water for 20 minutes

½ cup white balsamic vinegar

5 roasted cloves garlic (page 117)

1 cup olive oil

Kosher salt and freshly ground pepper to taste

• In a blender or food processor, combine all the ingredients and process until well blended. Sprinkle with salt and pepper. Let sit for about 20 minutes and serve. Or, cover and refrigerate for up to 3 days. Return to room temperature before serving.

VARIATION: Stir 1½ cups plain yogurt into this salsa to make a dip for fresh vegetables and plantain or yuca chips.

Grilled Yellow Tomato and Green Onion Salsa

I love the flavor of grilled vegetables. The beauty of grilling is that it's a very simple procedure that produces wonderful taste results. You can grill your tomatoes on an outdoor grill or in a hot grill pan. Or, you can achieve the same effect by baking them in a preheated 350°F oven for about 10 minutes. Just make sure you grill—or bake—your tomatoes skin-side down, or you'll spend more of your precious time cleaning than enjoying! This salsa blends nicely with red snapper or salmon.

MAKES ABOUT 2 ½ CUPS

3 yellow beefsteak tomatoes, halved

Olive oil for coating, plus ½ cup

Freshly ground pepper to taste

7 green onions

½ cup white balsamic vinegar

½ cup chopped fresh cilantro

• Prepare an outdoor grill or heat a grill pan over high heat. Coat the tomatoes with olive oil and sprinkle with pepper. Place the tomatoes, skin-side down, on the grill or in the grill pan and grill until the skin is nicely charred, or for about 10 minutes. Remove from heat and let cool to the touch. Chop coarsely. Coat the green onions with olive oil and grill for about 5 minutes on each side, or until softened. Remove from heat and let cool to the touch. Cut into fine dice.

•• In a large bowl, combine the tomatoes, green onions, the ½ cup oil, the vinegar, and cilantro. Stir well, using your hand or a wooden spoon. Let cool completely and serve.

Tomatillo, Cilantro, and Avocado Salsa

Mexican green tomatoes, known as *tomatillos* in Spanish, are a key ingredient in many Mexican salsas. Roasting them enhances their natural robust flavor. This guacamole-like salsa is great with chips.

MAKES ABOUT 3 CUPS

4 roasted tomatillos (page 117), each quartered

2 ripe Hass avocados, peeled, pitted, and coarsely chopped

1 red onion, diced

1 1/2 roasted poblano chiles (page 117), peeled, seeded, and diced

1/3 cup white balsamic vinegar

Juice of 1/2 lime

1 tablespoon olive oil

Kosher salt and freshly ground pepper to taste

2 tablespoons minced fresh cilantro

• In a large glass or ceramic bowl, combine the tomatillos and avocados. Gently stir in the red onion, chiles, vinegar, lime juice, oil, salt, and pepper (don't overdo it or the avocados will get mushy). Let sit for about 20 minutes, then stir in the cilantro and serve. Or, cover and refrigerate for up to 2 days. Return to room temperature and stir in the cilantro just before serving.

Mexican Salsa (*Salsa Mexicana*)

I first discovered chipotles—smoked jalapeño chiles—when I started working in New York. Now you won't catch me without a bottle of chipotle purée in my kitchen. It's fiery, but not to the point where it distracts from other key flavors. And you can always adjust the amount of chipotle according to your own taste. This smoky and sparky salsa is great with crunchy chips.

MAKES ABOUT 2 ½ CUPS

2 roasted tomatoes (page 117), coarsely chopped

1 roasted red onion (page 117), coarsely chopped

2 ripe Hass avocados, peeled, pitted, and coarsely chopped

Kosher salt and freshly ground pepper to taste

2 teaspoons white balsamic vinegar

1 tablespoon canola oil

1 tablespoon chipotle purée (page 120) or rocoto paste

Juice of 1 lime

2 tablespoons coarsely chopped fresh cilantro

• In a large bowl, combine the tomatoes, onion, and avocados. Toss gently. Gently stir in the salt, pepper, vinegar, oil, chipotle purée or rocoto paste, and lime juice. Let sit for about 20 minutes, then stir in the cilantro and serve. Or, cover and refrigerate for up to 1 day. Return to room temperature and stir in the cilantro just before serving.

Tomatillo and Roasted Yellow Pepper Salsa

Tomatillos are popular in two of my favorite cuisines: Mexican and Southwestern. They can be blanched, grilled, or eaten raw. Their flavor, which has subtle lemon, apple, and herbal notes, makes them ideal for salsas. In this salsa, I grill them with slightly sweet yellow bell peppers. I like to serve this salsa with pan-seared monkfish or simply with chips.

MAKES ABOUT 3 CUPS

9 roasted tomatillos (page 117), quartered

3 roasted yellow bell peppers (page 117), peeled, seeded, and julienned

1 tablespoon white balsamic vinegar

2 tablespoons extra-virgin olive oil

2 tablespoons chopped fresh cilantro

• In a large glass or ceramic bowl, combine the tomatillos, bell peppers, vinegar, and oil. Stir to blend. Let sit for about 20 minutes, then stir in the cilantro and serve. Or, cover and refrigerate for up to 2 days. Return to room temperature and stir in the cilantro just before serving.

Roasted Tomato and Tarragon Salsa

Tarragon, an anise-flavored herb widely used in classic French cooking, can be quite assertive, so it should be used *con cuidado*, with care. Here, the beautiful dark green narrow pointed leaves offer a sensual contrast to roasted red tomatoes. This salsa is ideally served with grilled steak or chicken.

MAKES ABOUT 2 CUPS

6 roasted plum tomatoes (page 117), coarsely chopped

1 tablespoon olive oil

1/4 cup white balsamic vinegar

1 teaspoon sherry wine vinegar

Kosher salt and freshly ground pepper to taste

Leaves from 1 bunch tarragon

• In a large bowl, combine all the ingredients except the tarragon. Stir to blend. Let sit for about 20 minutes, then stir in the tarragon and serve. Or, cover and refrigerate for up to 2 days. Return to room temperature and stir in the tarragon just before serving.

Pan-Roasted Tomato and Garbanzo Salsa

The mild nutlike flavor of garbanzo beans (also known as chickpeas) makes them ideal for combining with sweet pan-roasted tomatoes and rich roasted garlic. This is great on fresh Italian bread, as well as on fish and salads.

MAKES ABOUT 4 CUPS

2 red beefsteak tomatoes

1 teaspoon olive oil

7 roasted cloves garlic (page 117), peeled

2 cups cooked garbanzo beans (page 116), or 15 ounces canned beans, rinsed and drained

$^1/_2$ cup niçoise or kalamata olives, pitted and coarsely chopped

1 tablespoon minced fresh thyme

Kosher salt and freshly ground pepper to taste

Pinch of minced fresh chives

• Preheat the oven to 350°F. Cut the tomatoes in half crosswise. Place them, cut-side up, in a shallow baking pan. Drizzle the olive oil on top. Bake for about 8 minutes, or until softened. Remove from the oven and let cool to the touch. Chop coarsely.

• • In a large bowl, combine the tomatoes and all the remaining ingredients except the chives. Stir to blend. Let sit for about 20 minutes, then stir in the chives and serve. Or, cover and refrigerate for up to 3 days. Return to room temperature and stir in the chives just before serving.

Sun-Dried Tomato Rainbow Salsa

When I crave meat—which is pretty often—I like to try out different salsas with it. This one goes well with a nice steak, as well as grilled tuna. It also quickly dresses up a piece of crusty Italian bread or a bowl of steaming pasta.

MAKES ABOUT 3 CUPS

½ cup peeled pearl onions

½ cup dry-packed sun-dried tomatoes, soaked in hot water for 20 minutes, drained, and coarsely chopped

2 roasted red bell peppers (page 117), peeled, seeded, and coarsely chopped

1 roasted yellow bell pepper (page 117), peeled, seeded, and coarsely chopped

1 tablespoon minced fresh thyme

½ cup olive oil

¼ cup white balsamic vinegar

Pinch of ground cumin

Kosher salt and freshly ground pepper to taste

2 tablespoons coarsely chopped fresh chives

• Put the pearl onions in a strainer and submerge in a saucepan of boiling water for just 1 minute. Remove and drain. Let cool to the touch. Blanch the sun-dried tomatoes in the same way.

•• In a large bowl, combine the onions, the tomatoes, and all the remaining ingredients except the chives. Stir well. Let sit for about 20 minutes, then stir in the chives and serve. Or, cover and refrigerate for up to 3 days. Return to room temperature and stir in the chives just before serving.

Vegetable Salsas

(*Salsas del Jardín*)

Crunchy and smooth, colorful and rich, these salsas vibrate with summertime flavors. In salsas made with vegetables from asparagus to shiitakes, *salsas del jardín* celebrate your garden's bounty. Salsas are about contrast and balance. In these, the moist and rich orange flesh of pumpkin dances with crunchy, slightly salty roasted peanuts, and the mild flavor of potatoes marries beautifully with delicately sweet roasted red peppers.

Serve these salsas dolloped on main dishes—or on the side.

Opal Basil Chimichurri

The eggplant color of opal basil makes a nice change in traditionally green chimichurri, the "ketchup" of Argentina. This is a great marinade for steak (coat it with the sauce about 1 hour prior to grilling), or it can be used as a dipping sauce after the steak is grilled.

MAKES ABOUT 3 CUPS

1 bunch opal basil or regular basil, stemmed and coarsely chopped

1 bunch cilantro, stemmed and coarsely chopped

$3/4$ cup white balsamic vinegar

4 cloves garlic, minced

1 shallot, minced

$1/4$ cup canola oil

Kosher salt and freshly ground pepper to taste

• In a blender, combine the basil, cilantro, vinegar, garlic, and shallot. Purée until smooth. With the machine running, gradually add the oil. Add the salt and pepper. Let sit for about 20 minutes before serving. Or, cover and refrigerate for up to 5 days. Return to room temperature before serving.

Niçoise Olive and Cilantro Chimichurri

This intense sauce adds great flavor to chicken, meat, fish—and even crusty bread. My Sonora partner, Moe, uses it as a marinade for grilled chicken (which he then slices and serves on a green salad).

MAKES ABOUT 3 CUPS

1 cup niçoise or kalamata olives, pitted

1½ cups olive oil

1 cup white balsamic vinegar

1 teaspoon garlic oil (page 119)

1 roasted clove garlic (page 117), minced

Freshly ground black pepper to taste

1 bunch cilantro, stemmed and coarsely chopped

• In a large bowl, combine the olives, oil, vinegar, garlic, and pepper. Stir to blend. Let sit for about 20 minutes, then stir in the cilantro and serve. Or, cover and refrigerate for up to 3 days. Return to room temperature and stir in the cilantro just before serving.

Roasted Pepper and Basil Salsa

Maybe it's because of my Italian roots, but I can't live without fresh basil growing near me. I'm always finding new ways to combine this fragrant and tasty herb. This salsa can be served at room temperature as a spread for toasted sourdough or Italian bread, or heated to use as a sauce for fresh ravioli.

MAKES ABOUT 2½ CUPS

2 *each* roasted red and yellow bell peppers (page 117), peeled, seeded, and julienned

¼ cup white balsamic vinegar

½ cup olive oil

Salt and freshly ground pepper to taste

2 fresh basil leaves, stacked, rolled, and thinly sliced

• In a large bowl, combine the bell peppers, vinegar, oil, salt, and pepper. Stir to blend. Let sit for about 20 minutes, then stir in the basil and serve. Or, cover and refrigerate for up to 5 days. Return to room temperature and stir in the basil just before serving.

Niçoise Olive, Cilantro, and Thyme Tapenade

When I was just nineteen years old, I had a crash course in combining flavors under the tutelage of renowned French chef Michel Guérard. In his three-star kitchen in Eugénie-les-Bains, France, I spent a fabulous year learning not only the basics of classic French cooking but also the delicate art of marrying herbs with a variety of foods. This salsa brings together French ingredients (like niçoise olives and thyme) and Latin American ones (cilantro, red onion, and tomatoes). Whether you spread it on a piece of crusty French bread, dollop it on grilled fish, or lightly blanket it on grilled steak, you'll enjoy this versatile topping.

MAKES ABOUT 2½ CUPS

1/2 cup white balsamic vinegar

1/2 cup olive oil

1 tablespoon roasted garlic pulp (page 117)

1 roasted red onion (page 117), chopped

1 cup niçoise olives, pitted and finely diced

5 small plum tomatoes, peeled, seeded, and diced (page 118)

1 tablespoon minced fresh thyme

Kosher salt and freshly ground pepper to taste

1 cup fresh cilantro leaves, chopped

• In a large bowl, whisk the vinegar, oil, and garlic together. Add the red onion, olives, tomatoes, thyme, salt, and pepper. Stir well, using your hand or a wooden spoon. Let sit for about 20 minutes, then stir in the cilantro and serve. Or, cover and refrigerate for up to 2 days. Return to room temperature and stir in the cilantro just before serving.

Wild Mushroom Escabèche Salsa

An escabèche is traditionally thought of as a dish of poached or fried fish, served with a spicy marinade. Popular in southern France (where I first enjoyed it) and Spain, this dish is usually served cold. My escabèche salsa was inspired by my love of France, French cooking, and wild mushrooms! This gorgeous salsa is a natural with a grilled steak, but I also like to serve it on crusty rounds of toasted French bread.

MAKES ABOUT 2 CUPS

1 tablespoon unsalted butter

5 ounces shiitake mushrooms, stemmed and coarsely chopped

3 ounces oyster mushrooms, coarsely chopped

1 shallot, minced

3/4 cup dry sherry

1/2 cup chicken stock (page 118) or canned
 low-sodium chicken broth

Kosher salt and freshly ground pepper to taste

1/2 plum tomato, diced

1 teaspoon chopped fresh chives

• In a medium skillet or sauté pan, melt the butter over medium heat. Add the mushrooms and shallot. Sauté until they start to brown, 5 to 8 minutes. Add the sherry, increase heat to medium-high, and cook until the sherry is reduced by one-third. Add the stock or broth, bring to a boil, and remove from heat. Add the salt and pepper.

•• Pour the mixture into a large bowl and let cool to room temperature. Stir in the tomato. Let sit for about 20 minutes, then stir in the chives and serve. Or, cover and refrigerate for up to 3 days. Return to room temperature and stir in the chives just before serving.

Roasted Corn and Pickled Cucumber Salsa

This refreshing summertime salsa is great on grilled Chilean sea bass.

MAKES ABOUT 4 CUPS

2 cucumbers, halved lengthwise and seeded

1 cup water

1 cup white balsamic vinegar

Grated zest of 1 orange

1/2 cup apple cider

Kernels cut from 6 ears roasted corn (page 117)

Freshly ground pepper to taste

• Cut each cucumber half into 1/2-inch-thick half-moons.

•• In a large saucepan, combine the water, vinegar, cucumbers, and orange zest. Bring to a boil over medium heat and cook for 5 minutes. Remove from heat and let cool to room temperature. Transfer to a large bowl. Stir in all the remaining ingredients. Let sit for about 20 minutes before serving. Or, cover and refrigerate for up to 3 days. Return to room temperature before serving.

Roasted Beet and Carrot Salsa

This salsa is wonderful served over romaine lettuce. It's a great summertime salsa for barbecues!

MAKES ABOUT 2 ½ CUPS

6 unpeeled beets, cut into wedges

Olive oil for coating

Kosher salt and freshly ground pepper to taste

2 carrots, peeled and cut into half-moons

1 cup dried mango, diced

$^1/_3$ cup sherry wine vinegar

$^1/_3$ cup canola oil

Pinch of ground cinnamon

• Preheat the oven to 350°F. Lightly coat the beet wedges with olive oil and place them in an ovenproof pan. Sprinkle with salt and pepper. Cover with aluminum foil and bake for 45 minutes to 1 hour, or until tender. Let cool to room temperature, then peel.

•• Meanwhile, cook the carrots in salted boiling water for about 5 minutes, or until crisp-tender. Immediately drain and let cool to room temperature.

••• In a large bowl, combine the beets, carrots, and all the remaining ingredients. Serve immediately. Or, cover and refrigerate for up to 3 days. Return to room temperature before serving.

Pumpkin and Roasted Peanut Salsa

When my coauthor, Arlen Gargagliano, lived in Peru, she loved to visit the *mercado central*, Lima's famous open-air market. Among all the vendors that would call out for her to buy their gorgeously stacked fruits and vegetables, there was one that she especially liked: Doña Ana, whose specialty was *zapallo* (pumpkin). Every week Doña Ana would call Arlen over and, in her heavy Quechuan accent, tell her what she could make with the beautiful *zapallo*. From soups and salsas to desserts, pumpkin has offered the New World its gifts for centuries. This salsa is a gorgeous complement to a salad of frisée lettuce.

MAKES ABOUT 4½ CUPS

1½ pounds sugar pie pumpkin, peeled, seeded, and diced (about 4 cups)

½ cup sherry wine vinegar

½ cup white balsamic vinegar

½ cup (3½ ounces) grated panela (page 11) or packed brown sugar

1 cup roasted unsalted peanuts, coarsely chopped

Kosher salt and freshly ground pepper to taste

½ cup dried mango, diced

• Cook the pumpkin in salted boiling water for 5 minutes. Immediately drain and rinse with cold water.

•• Meanwhile, in a small saucepan, combine the vinegars and panela or brown sugar. Cook over medium heat for about 10 minutes, or until reduced by about three-fourths. Let cool to room temperature.

••• In a large bowl, combine the pumpkin, vinegar mixture, and all the remaining ingredients. Stir to blend. Let sit for about 20 minutes before serving. Or, cover and refrigerate for up to 3 days. Return to room temperature before serving.

Roasted Corn and Black Bean Salsa

Roasting corn brings out its natural sweetness, which balances so nicely with the hearty black beans in this salsa. I like to make this in large amounts for two reasons: One, it goes quickly; and two, it keeps for several days (but if you are making it ahead of time, add the avocado and cilantro as close to serving time as possible). We've used this to top quesadillas in Sonora, as a topping for mesclun or other greens, and to dig into with mixed chips. You can also stir it into room-temperature white rice for a colorful summertime rice salad.

MAKES ABOUT 9 CUPS

3 cups cooked black beans (page 115), or 30 ounces
  canned beans, drained and rinsed

Kernels cut from 8 ears roasted corn (page 117), 4 cups

1 pound plum tomatoes, diced (about 2 cups)

2 teaspoons ají amarillo or chipotle purée (page 120)

1/3 cup white balsamic vinegar

1/4 cup olive oil

Juice of 1/2 lime

Kosher salt and freshly ground pepper to taste

1 avocado, peeled, pitted, and diced

1 cup chopped fresh cilantro

• In a large bowl, combine the black beans, corn kernels, and tomatoes. Stir in all the remaining ingredients except the avocado and cilantro. Let sit for about 20 minutes, then gently stir in the avocado and cilantro and serve. Or, cover and refrigerate for up to 3 days. Return to room temperature and gently stir in the avocado and cilantro just before serving.

Roasted Eggplant and Yellow Pepper Salsa

Though I grew up in Colombia, my grandparents came from Italy. Maybe that's where my love of eggplant—among other Italian treats—stems from. Recently, I've discovered Japanese eggplant. This salsa is great on grilled chicken, or a bed of cooked or raw spinach.

MAKES ABOUT 6 CUPS

8 roasted baby or Japanese eggplants (page 117)

2 roasted yellow bell peppers (page 117) peeled, seeded, and julienned

2 pounds plum tomatoes, diced (about 4 cups)

1/4 cup olive oil

1/4 cup white balsamic vinegar

1/2 cup kalamata olives, pitted and halved

2 tablespoons chopped fresh cilantro

• Halve the eggplants and scoop out the meat. In a large bowl, combine the eggplants, bell peppers, and tomatoes. Stir in the oil, vinegar, and olives. Let sit for about 20 minutes, then stir in the cilantro and serve. Or, cover and refrigerate for up to 2 days. Return to room temperature and stir in the cilantro just before serving.

Grilled Asparagus and Blue Cheese Salsa

The rich blue cheese is balanced by the flavor of grilled asparagus. This refreshing combination is a great topping for a portobello burger— or a hamburger—on a bun.

MAKES ABOUT 3½ CUPS

1 bunch asparagus

½ teaspoon garlic oil (page 119)

Freshly ground pepper to taste

2 cups crumbled blue cheese

½ roasted red bell pepper (page 117), peeled, seeded, and diced

½ cup olive oil

½ cup white balsamic vinegar

Juice of ½ lime

Kosher salt to taste

1 teaspoon chopped fresh chives

• Light a fire in a charcoal grill, preheat a gas grill, or heat a grill pan over high heat. Coat the asparagus with the garlic oil and sprinkle with pepper. Grill the asparagus for 2 to 3 minutes on each side, or until slightly softened. Let cool to room temperature and dice.

•• In a large bowl, combine the asparagus, blue cheese, and bell pepper. Stir in the oil, vinegar, lime juice, and salt. Let sit for about 20 minutes, then stir in the chives and serve. Or, cover and refrigerate for up to 2 days. Return to room temperature and stir in the chives just before serving.

Shiitake Mushroom Chimichurri

I've always been a mushroom fan; I love morels and portobellos. But when I started working in New York, I discovered the wonders of shiitake mushrooms. Originally from Japan and Korea, these delicious mushrooms are sold in both dried and fresh form throughout the United States. Though they can be quite pricey, fresh shiitakes make this salsa an excellent one for marinating—or topping—steaks.

MAKES ABOUT 2 CUPS

4 ounces shiitake mushrooms, stemmed

Olive oil for coating, plus ½ cup

1 teaspoon minced garlic

½ teaspoon minced fresh thyme

¼ teaspoon dried oregano

1 shallot, minced

Juice of ½ lime

Pinch of red pepper flakes

¼ cup balsamic vinegar

Kosher salt and freshly ground black pepper to taste

1 tablespoon chopped fresh cilantro

• Preheat the oven to 500°F. Lightly coat the mushrooms with oil and put them on a baking sheet. Sprinkle the garlic, thyme, and oregano on top. Bake for 5 minutes, or until slightly toasted. Remove and let cool to room temperature. Coarsely chop.

•• In a blender, combine all the remaining ingredients except the cilantro. Add the mushrooms and pulse just until mixed. Let sit for about 20 minutes, then stir in the cilantro and serve. Or, cover and refrigerate for up to 3 days. Return to room temperature and stir in the cilantro just before serving.

Red Bliss and Bell Pepper Salsa

This is one of those salsas that could double as a side dish. Just make sure you don't overcook the potatoes, or they'll get mushy. I love this with chips—but you could also spoon it on top of a spinach or mixed green salad.

MAKES ABOUT 3½ CUPS

6 medium Red Bliss potatoes (about 1½ pounds)

Kosher salt to taste

2 roasted red bell peppers (page 117), peeled, seeded, and julienned

2 roasted poblano chiles (page 117), peeled, seeded, and diced

⅓ cup olive oil

¼ cup white balsamic vinegar

Freshly ground pepper to taste

2 tablespoons chopped fresh cilantro

1 tablespoon minced fresh thyme

• Put the potatoes in a medium, heavy saucepan and add cold water to cover. Add salt. Cover, bring to a boil, reduce heat to a simmer, and cook for 15 minutes, or until easily pierced with a knife. Drain and let cool to room temperature. Cut the potatoes into ¼-inch dice.

•• In a large bowl, combine the potatoes, bell peppers, and chiles. Add the oil, vinegar, and pepper. Gently stir. Let sit for about 20 minutes, then stir in the cilantro and thyme and serve. Or, cover and refrigerate for up to 5 days. Return to room temperature and stir in the cilantro and thyme just before serving.

Chile Salsas

(*Salsas de Chiles*)

Chiles have played a starring role in the world's cuisine for centuries. Though there are more than two hundred varieties of chiles, over one hundred of them are indigenous to Mexico. Needless to say, chiles grace a variety of Mexican dishes—and, of course, salsas.

Salsas de chiles are sparky. They add ranging levels of heat to the vegetables and fruits they're paired with. *¡No tengan miedo!* Don't be afraid! There is a chile salsa out there for you. Go easy at first; remember, you can control the heat by easing up on the quantity of chiles. Once you begin your spicy adventure and start matching up salsas with their complementary dishes, you'll yearn to keep exploring.

Roasted Jalapeño and Tomato Salsa

This slightly smoky salsa reminds me of the sultry breezes of summer. Scoop it up with crispy *patacones*, plantain chips, and accompany with ice-cold Negra Modelo (a tasty Mexican beer). It's also an ideal topping for grilled fish such as sea bass or trout.

MAKES ABOUT 2 CUPS

3 tablespoons extra-virgin olive oil

4 plum tomatoes, diced

8 roasted cloves garlic (page 117), minced

1 red onion, diced

Kosher salt and freshly ground pepper to taste

2 tablespoons white balsamic vinegar

2 roasted jalapeño chiles (page 117), peeled, seeded, and diced

2 teaspoons chopped fresh cilantro

• In a medium saucepan over medium heat, heat 2 tablespoons of the oil. Sauté the tomatoes and garlic for about 2 minutes, or until the tomatoes soften slightly. Scrape into a medium bowl.

• • In the same pan, heat the remaining 1 tablespoon oil. Add the onion, salt, and pepper. Sauté for about 2 minutes, or until softened. Add to the tomato mixture. Let cool to room temperature.

• • • Stir in the vinegar and chiles. Let sit for about 20 minutes, then stir in the cilantro and serve. Or, cover and refrigerate for up to 2 days. Return to room temperature and stir in the cilantro just before serving.

Avocado and Serrano Salsa

The luscious and creamy flesh of the avocado makes it an ideal partner for a variety of chiles, and it also helps to balance their heat. Though the serrano is not too *picante*, it does have a bite. But even people who don't like spicy food like this very easy-to-prepare salsa.

MAKES ABOUT 2½ CUPS

½ cucumber, seeded and diced

2 ripe Hass avocados, peeled, pitted, and coarsely chopped

1 red onion, diced

2 serrano chiles, finely chopped

Kosher salt and freshly ground pepper to taste

Juice of ½ lime

• In a large glass or ceramic bowl, combine the cucumber, avocados, onion, and chiles. Toss well. Gently stir in the salt, pepper, and lime juice (take care, or the avocado will get mushy). Serve immediately. Or, cover and refrigerate for up to 1 day. Return to room temperature before serving.

Roasted Jalapeño and Citrus Salsa

This Yucatan-style salsa is *una belleza*, a beauty! It packs a bite and is ideally served on grilled fish such as red snapper, sea bass, or tilapia (also called St. Peter's fish). To peel and cut the citrus into segments, see page 118.

MAKES ABOUT 2 CUPS

2 roasted jalapeño chiles (page 117), peeled, seeded, and diced

Grated zest of 1 orange

3 oranges, peeled and cut into segments

1 grapefruit, peeled and cut into segments

1 lemon, peeled and cut into segments

1 lime, peeled and cut into segments

2 tablespoons soybean oil

Kosher salt to taste

1 tablespoon sugar

1 tablespoon ¼-inch diagonally cut green onion tops

• In a large bowl, combine the chiles, orange zest, and citrus segments. Stir in the oil, salt, and sugar. Let sit for about 20 minutes, then stir in the green onions and serve. Or, cover and refrigerate for up to 3 days. Return to room temperature and stir in the green onions just before serving.

Serrano and Roasted Vine-Ripened Tomato Salsa

The sharp bite of this salsa is not for everyone, but if you like serrano chiles, it's definitely for you! This salsa works well with any kind of chip, and *una cerveza bien fría* (an ice-cold beer).

MAKES ABOUT 2 CUPS

4 roasted vine-ripened tomatoes (page 117), about 1 pound

5 roasted green serrano chiles (page 117)

2 tablespoons olive oil

2 tablespoons white balsamic vinegar

Kosher salt and freshly ground pepper to taste

• Coarsely chop the tomatoes and chiles. In a large bowl, combine the tomatoes, chiles, oil, vinegar, salt, and pepper. Let sit for about 20 minutes before serving. Or, cover and refrigerate for up to 3 days. Return to room temperature before serving.

Roasted Poblano Chile, Tomato, and Avocado Salsa

Simple, clean, and tasty, with a bit of heat, this salsa is should be served with ice-cold Aguilas (a flavorful Colombian beer) and chips as you're lighting the charcoal for a summer barbecue.

MAKES ABOUT 5 CUPS

3 roasted poblano chiles (page 117), peeled, seeded, and diced

3 red beefsteak tomatoes, diced

2 ripe Hass avocados, peeled, pitted, and coarsely chopped

2 teaspoons rocoto paste or chipotle purée (page 120)

Juice of 1/2 lime

Kosher salt and freshly ground pepper to taste

• In a large bowl, combine the chiles, tomatoes, and avocados. Stir to blend. Gently stir in the remaining ingredients, being careful not to stir too much (or the avocado will get mushy). Let sit for about 20 minutes, before serving. Or, cover and refrigerate for up to 1 day. Return to room temperature before serving.

Bean Salsas

(*Salsas de Frijoles*)

Versatile and soothing, beans can take on the flavors of the foods they're cooked with while maintaining their individuality. Whether it's the nutty flesh of garbanzos or hearty lentils, beans contribute both backdrop and contrast.

Salsas de frijoles are comforting. They balance a variety of dishes, and hold their own atop beds of rice. You'll love the flexibility of these nutritious, tasty salsas.

Garbanzo, Roasted Pepper, and Green Onion Salsa

The Spaniards knew what they were doing when they developed the custom of going "*de tapas*." The appetizer-sized treats, served in bars such as those around Madrid's famous Plaza Mayor, were traditionally served on tiny plates that covered, *taparon*, the glasses of wine or beer that accompanied them—hence the name *tapas*. While going "*de tapas*" one night, I discovered a variation of this garbanzo salsa. Though I especially enjoy this salsa on grilled or roasted leg of lamb, I'm sure you'll find your own complement for it.

MAKES ABOUT 3 CUPS

Kernels cut from 2 ears roasted corn (page 117),
  or 1 cup roasted corn kernels (page 117)

1 1/2 cups cooked garbanzo beans (page 116),
  or 15 ounces canned beans, drained and rinsed

1 roasted red bell pepper (page 117), peeled, seeded,
  and coarsely chopped

1 tablespoon chopped fresh thyme

1/4 cup olive oil

2 tablespoons balsamic vinegar

1/2 red onion, julienned

1/2 cup thinly sliced green onions, including pale green parts

1 hard-cooked egg, shredded or finely chopped

Kosher salt and freshly ground pepper to taste

1/4 cup chopped fresh cilantro

• In a large bowl, combine all the ingredients except the cilantro. Stir well, using your hand or a wooden spoon. Let sit for about 20 minutes, then stir in the cilantro and serve. Or, cover and refrigerate for up to 3 days. Return to room temperature and stir in the cilantro just before serving.

Lima Bean, Kalamata Olive, and Roasted Garlic Salsa

Lima beans, named after Lima, Peru, are great in soups and salads—as well as in this salsa. I like to serve it with fresh pasta.

MAKES ABOUT 1½ CUPS

1 cup cooked lima beans (page 116)

½ roasted red bell pepper (page 117), peeled, seeded, and julienned

1 roasted clove garlic (page 117), minced

¼ cup kalamata olives, pitted

Freshly ground pepper to taste

2 tablespoons minced fresh cilantro

• In a large bowl, combine the beans, bell pepper, garlic, and olives. Gently stir, with a wooden spoon or your hand, just until blended. Stir in the pepper. Let sit for about 20 minutes, then stir in the cilantro and serve. Or, cover and refrigerate for up to 3 days. Return to room temperature and stir in the cilantro just before serving.

Lentil, Pan-Roasted Onion, and Niçoise Olive Salsa

I love lentils in everything from soups to salsas because they are so flavorful. This salsa uses black beluga lentils, which are very popular in South Asia. Their soft, earthy flavor and texture works well with roasted red onion and red bell pepper. The flavors and colors of this salsa pair well with Chilean sea bass.

MAKES ABOUT 4 CUPS

1 red onion, sliced and separated into rings

Kosher salt to taste

1 cup cooked black beluga or green lentils (page 115)

1 cup niçoise olives, pitted

1 large roasted red bell pepper (page 117), peeled, seeded, and diced

1/2 cup olive oil

1/4 cup white balsamic vinegar

Pinch of ground cumin

Freshly ground pepper to taste

3 bunches mâche (field lettuce)

• Preheat the oven to 350°F. Spread the onion rings out on a lightly oiled baking sheet and sprinkle with kosher salt. Roast for 10 to 12 minutes, or until nicely browned around the edges.

•• In a large bowl, combine the lentils, olives, and bell pepper. Stir to blend. Stir in all the remaining ingredients except the mâche. Let sit for about 20 minutes, then add the mâche and serve. Or, cover and refrigerate for up to 3 days. Return to room temperature and add the mâche just before serving.

Bean Tapenade Salsa

Cooking is like *bailando*, dancing. With dancing, you learn the steps, get comfortable, and then you start to let the music carry you away. In cooking, your style comes from experimenting with new flavors and taste combinations. I was just nineteen when, under the tutelage of famous chef Michel Guérard in beautiful southern France, I learned about combining flavors I was previously unfamiliar with. I learned about things like tapenade: traditionally a thick paste made from capers, anchovies, ripe olives, lemon juice, and olive oil. This salsa is my own interpretation of tapenade, made with ingredients from my native Colombia and the Mediterranean region. I like to serve it on top of thick slices of roast pork, but it's also great just spooned onto chips—or even topping a salad.

MAKES ABOUT 3½ CUPS

1 cup cooked white beans (page 115)

3 roasted red bell peppers (page 117), peeled, seeded, and julienned

1 cup roasted corn kernels (page 117)

1 cup kalamata olives, pitted and halved lengthwise

½ cup olive oil

½ cup white balsamic vinegar

Kosher salt and freshly ground pepper to taste

2 tablespoons chopped fresh cilantro

• In a large bowl, combine the beans, bell peppers, and corn. Stir in all the remaining ingredients except the cilantro. Let sit for about 20 minutes, then stir in the cilantro and serve. Or, cover and refrigerate for up to 5 days. Return to room temperature and stir in the cilantro just before serving.

Dessert Salsas

(*Salsas de Postres*)

Sweet, sensual, and soothing in so many ways, *salsas de postres* are the equivalent of an incredible late-night kiss. A good dessert salsa should leave you smiling, with the desire for more.

These fresh and colorful salsas are simple and delicate. Whether used as toppings for dulce de leche (or your favorite) ice cream, or thick slices of pound cake, *salsas de postres* are both light and satisfying.

Blueberry, Papaya, and Toasted-Almond Salsa

July, a steamy month in New York City, is also the time that I like to leave Manhattan and go blueberry picking with my family. My motto for blueberry picking has always been "Pick two, eat two," but if we keep at it long enough, we manage to collect a nice amount. Aside from making blueberry muffins and pancakes, I like to keep some berries aside for salsa. This nutty salsa goes well on top of dulce de leche ice cream or shortcake.

MAKES ABOUT 3 ½ CUPS

3/4 cup fresh blueberries

1/2 papaya, peeled, seeded, and diced (about 2 cups)

1/2 cup almonds, toasted (page 118)

2 ounces Frangelico (hazelnut-flavored liqueur)

Juice of 1 lime

1 tablespoon thinly sliced fresh mint leaves

• In a large bowl, combine the blueberries and papaya. Stir in the almonds, Frangelico, and lime juice. Let sit for about 10 minutes, then stir in the mint and serve. Or, cover and refrigerate for up to 1 day. Return to room temperature and stir in the mint just before serving.

Blackberry, Aguardiente, and Papaya Salsa

Colores fabulosos! A great salsa to serve on top of vanilla ice cream.

MAKES ABOUT 5 CUPS

1/2 papaya, peeled, seeded, and diced

2 cups fresh blackberries

1 mango, peeled, cut from the pit, and finely diced

1/3 cup aguardiente (Colombian brandy) or Greek ouzo

• In a large bowl, combine all the ingredients. Stir to blend. Serve immediately. Or, cover and refrigerate for up to 3 days. Return to room temperature before serving.

Peach and Toasted-Macadamia Salsa

The macadamia tree, grown originally for ornamental purposes, has traveled from Australia to California. Most of us associate it with its current largest exporter, Hawaii. The flavor of macadamia nuts reminds me of the *avellana*, a hazelnut I grew up with in Colombia. Like the hazelnut, the rich and buttery macadamia nut is as good in both sweet and savory salsas. In fact, though I serve this salsa atop my favorite dulce de leche ice cream, I would also serve it on top of grilled chicken.

MAKES ABOUT 3½ CUPS

1 cup macadamia nuts, toasted (page 118)

4 ripe peaches, peeled, pitted, and coarsely chopped

Grated zest of ½ orange

½ cup white balsamic vinegar

½ cup Grand Marnier

• Coarsely chop the nuts. In a large glass or ceramic bowl, combine the nuts, peaches, and orange zest. Toss well. Stir in the vinegar and Grand Marnier. Serve immediately. Or, cover and refrigerate for up to 2 days. Return to room temperature before serving. Or, fold into ice cream and freeze.

Three-Berry Aguardiente Salsa

I was initiated into the world of *flambé* as a sixteen-year-old working part-time at Larry Forgione's famous River Café in Brooklyn. Flambé, which literally means "flamed" in French, is a dramatic method of food presentation in which certain dishes are sprinkled with liquor and ignited just prior to serving. Try your hand at serving this salsa flambé style. Serve it on top of your favorite ice cream or slices of fresh pound cake.

MAKES ABOUT 4½ CUPS

2 cups fresh strawberries, hulled and quartered

1 cup fresh blackberries

1 cup fresh blueberries

5 tablespoons aguardiente (Colombian brandy) or Greek ouzo

1 tablespoon sugar, or to taste

5 fresh mint leaves, stacked, rolled, and cut into thin shreds

• In a medium saucepan, combine the strawberries, blackberries, and blueberries. Add the aguardiente or ouzo and sugar. Stir to blend. Cook over medium heat for 2 minutes. Using a long-handled match, light the liquid. *Cuidado!* Careful! The flames will jump! After the flames subside, stir in the mint and serve immediately.

Dulce de Leche Fruit Salsa

Dulce de leche, caramelized milk, has been a favorite of mine for as long as I can remember. This smooth, creamy, toffeelike sweet can be used in many ways: as a topping for ice cream, a base for a fondue, or a filling for pastries and cookies—to name just a few. This dessert salsa is ideally served on top of pound cake, vanilla ice cream, or both.

MAKES ABOUT 2 CUPS

1 cup dulce de leche (page 120)

½ cup heavy cream

2 cups fresh strawberries, hulled and quartered

2 cups fresh raspberries

1 teaspoon Cointreau

• In a medium saucepan, combine the dulce de leche and heavy cream. Cook over low heat, stirring constantly with a wooden spoon, until well blended. Increase heat to medium and bring to a boil. Add the berries and Cointreau and cook for just 30 seconds. Remove from heat and serve immediately.

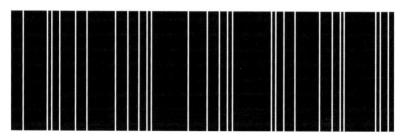

Basics

Beans

Whether black, white, Navy, pea, kidney, pink, or pinto, they all belong to the *Phaseolus vulgaris* group of the legume family. Cultivated for over four thousand years, beans (along with corn, squash, and chiles) are one of the four primary foods of the New World. I usually do not soak most beans, but it may be necessary if your beans have been shelved for a long time. Be sure not to add salt until the beans are tender.

MAKES ABOUT 4 CUPS

2 cups (1 pound) dried beans
6 to 8 cups chicken stock (page 118), canned low-salt
  chicken broth, or water
Kosher salt to taste

• Rinse and pick over the beans. Put in a large saucepan and add stock, broth, or water to cover by 2 inches. Bring to a simmer, cover, and cook for 1½ to 2 hours, or until tender but not mushy. Add salt. Use now, or let cool, cover, and refrigerate for up to 5 days.

Black Beluga Lentils

Lentils, which have been eaten for thousands of years, are easy to cook and very nutritious. I like their earthy flavor, which blends well with so many savory and sweet foods (as in Pear and Lentil Salsa, page 24).

MAKES ABOUT 3 CUPS

2 cups (1 pound) dried black beluga or green lentils
6 to 8 cups chicken stock (page 118), canned low-salt
  chicken broth, or water
Kosher salt to taste

• Rinse and pick over the lentils. Put in a large saucepan and add stock, broth, or water to cover by 2 inches. Bring to a simmer and cook, uncovered, for 30 to 40 minutes, or until tender but firm. Add salt. Use now, or let cool, cover, and refrigerate for up to 5 days.

Garbanzo Beans

Though they are native to the Middle East, thanks to the Spanish and Portuguese we have garbanzos in the New World. These hard, round, beige peas need to be soaked overnight before cooking.

MAKES ABOUT 4 CUPS

2 cups (1 pound) garbanzo beans (chickpeas)
6 to 8 cups chicken stock (page 118), canned low-salt
** chicken broth, or water**
Kosher salt to taste

• Rinse and pick over the beans. Soak overnight in cold water to cover by 2 inches. Drain.

•• Put the beans in a large saucepan and add stock, broth, or water to cover by 2 inches. Bring to a simmer and cook, uncovered, for 1 to 1½ hours, or until tender but firm. Add salt. Use now, or let cool, cover, and refrigerate for up to 5 days.

Lima Beans

Lima beans were originally cultivated in Lima, Peru. Today they have made their way into all kinds of dishes, including succotash and even salads.

MAKES ABOUT 1 CUP

½ cup dried lima beans
3 cups chicken stock (page 118), canned low-salt chicken broth, or water
Kosher salt to taste

• Rinse and pick over the beans. Soak in water to cover by 2 inches for about 2 hours. Drain.

•• In a medium saucepan, bring the stock, broth, or water to a boil. Add the beans, reduce heat to a simmer and cook, uncovered, for about 1 hour, or until tender but firm. Add salt. Serve now, or let cool, cover, and refrigerate for up to 5 days.

Quinoa

• To prepare quinoa, rinse using a mesh strainer or by running water over. Drain excess water. Place in a saucepan and add water (2 cups water to 1 cup quinoa) and bring to a boil. Cook in salted boiling water for about 10 minutes, or until al dente. You'll see that the grains have turned transparent and the spiral-like germ has separated.

MAKES 3 CUPS.

Roasted Vegetables

ROASTED CORN: Peel back the husks and remove the corn silk. Fold the husks back over the corn, place the ears in a preheated 375°F oven, and roast, rotating every few minutes, for 15 to 20 minutes, or until the kernels are lightly browned.

ROASTED CORN KERNELS: Toss fresh or thawed frozen corn kernels with a bit of garlic in a very hot skillet until lightly browned.

ROASTED JAPANESE EGGPLANTS: Cut the eggplants in half lengthwise. Coat with olive oil and sprinkle with freshly ground pepper. Roast in a preheated 375°F oven until softened and lightly browned, about 8 to 10 minutes. Scoop out the flesh.

ROASTED GARLIC CLOVES: Peel single cloves of garlic, place on a square of aluminum foil, sprinkle with kosher salt, and wrap in the foil. Roast in a preheated 350°F oven for 12 to 15 minutes, or until very soft.

ROASTED GARLIC PULP: Remove the loose skin from a whole head of garlic. Wrap the garlic in aluminum foil and roast in a preheated 350°F oven for 45 to 60 minutes, or until very soft. To remove, cut off the top of the bulb and squeeze the pulp out of the skin.

ROASTED TOMATOES: Core the tomatoes and cut them in half crosswise. Squeeze gently to remove most of the seeds. Place on a broiler pan or baking sheet, cut-side down. Roast under a preheated broiler, as close to the heat source as possible, for 6 to 8 minutes, or until browned and blistered all over. Peel off the skin. Don't worry if it doesn't all come off; charred skin adds great flavor. Or, roast whole tomatoes on an oiled grill or in an oiled grill pan over medium heat for 8 to 10 minutes, turning them periodically with tongs.

ROASTED TOMATILLOS: Husk and rinse the tomatillos. Remove the stems. Coat with olive oil. Place on a baking sheet and sprinkle with kosher salt and freshly ground pepper. Roast in a preheated 375°F oven for 10 to 15 minutes, or until lightly browned.

ROASTED ONIONS: Remove the outer dry skin. Coat the onions with olive oil, place on a baking sheet, and sprinkle with kosher salt. Roast in a preheated 350°F oven for about 45 minutes, or until lightly browned.

ROASTED AND PEELED PEPPERS AND CHILES: Spike a whole pepper or chile with a long fork and hold it directly over a gas flame, or place on a grill over hot coals, or in a very hot cast-iron skillet. Turn until it is charred on all sides. Or, to roast under a broiler: Cut the pepper or chile in half lengthwise. Core and remove the seeds and ribs. Lay the pepper or chile skin-side up, on a baking sheet. Roast under a preheated broiler, as close to the heat source as possible, 2 to 4 minutes each side, until the skin is charred.

(CONTINUED)

You may want to use kitchen gloves when handling the chiles; if you have a small cut, those little seeds can burn. Place the pepper or chile in a plastic or paper bag and close the bag. Let sit for about 10 minutes, or until cool to the touch. Pull out the stem and rub off the black skin. Cut the pepper or chile in half and remove the seeds with your hands—don't use water or you will lose all those wonderful oils you worked so hard to get. Use right away, or submerge in olive oil, cover tightly, and refrigerate for up to 3 days.

TOASTING NUTS: Place the nuts on a baking sheet and toast in a preheated 350°F oven for 3 to 5 minutes, or until lightly browned.

PEELING AND SEEDING TOMATOES: Submerge tomatoes in boiling water for about 5 seconds, then transfer to ice water. Peel off the skin. To seed, halve the tomatoes and shake them upside down over a sink.

PEELING AND SEGMENTING CITRUS FRUIT: Using a large knife, cut off the top and bottom of the fruit down to the flesh. Stand the fruit on end and cut off the peel in strips from top to bottom, cutting down to the flesh. Holding the fruit over a bowl, cut between the membranes to release the segments.

Chicken Stock (*Caldo de Pollo*)

Any chef will tell you that a good chicken stock is a key ingredient in many dishes. This is the recipe for the stock that you'll find simmering in my restaurants—and in my *casa*.

MAKES ABOUT 6 CUPS

> 1 small chicken (about 3 1/2 pounds), quartered
> 1 teaspoon kosher salt
> 1 large celery stalk with leaves, coarsely chopped
> 2 carrots, peeled and coarsely chopped
> 1 onion, coarsely chopped
> 1 bay leaf
> 1 bunch cilantro, stemmed and coarsely chopped
> Cloves from 1 small head garlic

• Rinse the chicken well and trim off all excess fat. Put it in a large stockpot and add water to cover. Add the salt and bring to a boil. Skim off any fat or scum that rises to the surface. Add all the remaining ingredients and reduce heat to low. Simmer uncovered, until the chicken is fork-tender, about 2 hours, skimming occasionally as necessary. Add water as needed to keep the chicken covered.

•• Pour the stock through a fine-mesh sieve into another pot or a large bowl, pressing on the solids with the back of a large spoon to release the liquid. Spoon off the fat that rises to the top. You can make the stock even clearer by straining it through paper towels. Let cool to room temperature. Cover and refrigerate overnight. Remove the congealed fat from the stock. Store in the refrigerator for up to 3 days, or freeze for up to 3 months.

Caipirinha

The caipirinha, the national drink of Brazil, is a tasty and powerful combination of fresh lime juice, sugar, and cachaça, Brazilian rum. Not only is this cocktail samba-inspiring, it's also a great flavor enhancer for salsas. When you need to prepare caipirinha for a recipe, such as for my Pineapple and Caipirinha Salsa (page 34), make a few extra so that you and your friend(s) can enjoy sipping them as well.

SERVES 1

2 limes, scrubbed and each cut into 8 wedges
2 to 3 teaspoons superfine sugar
2 ounces (¼ cup) cachaça or white rum
Ice cubes

• Put the lime wedges in a cocktail shaker and add the sugar. Using a pestle or the end of a wooden spoon, mash the limes and sugar together. Add the cachaça or rum and several ice cubes. Shake well and strain into a glass filled with ice.

Garlic Oil

You'll find so many ways to use this oil, from adding it to salsas and vinaigrettes to drizzling it on top of grilled fish and even crusty French bread!

MAKES 1 CUP

1 tablespoon roasted garlic pulp (page 117)
1 cup canola oil
Kosher salt and freshly ground pepper to taste

• In a blender or food processor, purée the garlic. With the machine running, gradually add the oil and process just until mixed. Stir in the salt and pepper. Use now, or cover tightly and refrigerate for up to 3 days. Mix well before serving.

Chipotle Purée

I keep this in a squeeze bottle in my restaurants and at home. Empty a 13 ½-ounce can of chipotles en adobo into a blender or food processor and purée until smooth. Cover and store in the refrigerator for up to 6 months.

MAKES 1 CUP

Dulce de Leche

In Latin America, this smooth caramelized milk was blanketing cookies and stuffing pastries for years before Häagen-Dazs introduced its Dulce de Leche ice cream. Here are two recipes: The first is the one my *abuelita* (grandmother) used, and the other is a less labor-intensive method.

GRANDMA'S DULCE DE LECHE

MAKES ABOUT 2 CUPS

> **4 cups whole milk**
> **2 cups sugar**
> **¹/₄ teaspoon baking soda**
> **Pinch of ground cinnamon**

• In a large saucepan, combine all the ingredients. Cook over medium heat without stirring for 15 to 20 minutes. Reduce heat to low and cook for 25 to 30 minutes, stirring constantly with a wooden spoon. When the mixture thickens so much that you can see the bottom of the pan as you stir, remove from heat. Let cool completely. Cover and store in the refrigerator for up to 2 weeks.

EASY DULCE DE LECHE

MAKES 1 ¾ CUPS

> **One 14-ounce can sweetened condensed milk**

• Put the unopened can in a stockpot and add cold water to cover by 2 inches. Bring the water to a moderate boil and cook for 1 hour and 45 minutes. Make sure you frequently check the water to make sure it is always covering the can. Do not let cook for more than 2 hours; not only will you overcook the dulce de leche, you will also run the risk of exploding the can (which, I am happy to report, has never happened in my family, though we have been making dulce de leche for many, many years). Using tongs, occasionally turn the can over to stir the milk.

• • Remove the can from the water after the above time and let cool completely before opening. Transfer the caramelized milk to an airtight container and store in the refrigerator for up to 2 weeks.

Sources

You'll probably be able to find most of the ingredients for these recipes in your local supermarket. But just in case, here are some sources that offer a convenient way of finding special foods. Also, it's a lot of fun to go through these catalogs; I'm sure you'll find some other ingredients to add to your pantry.

DEAN AND DELUCA
560 Broadway
New York, NY 10012
Phone: (877) 826-9246
Web site: www.deandeluca.com
CHILES, DRIED BEANS, AND MORE.

EARTHY DELIGHTS
1161 East Clark Road, Suite 260
DeWitt, MI 48820
Phone: (800) 367-4709
or (517) 668-2402
Fax: (517) 668-1213
Web site: www.earthy.com
GRAINS, BEANS, LENTILS, AND MORE.

FRIEDA'S
4465 Corporate Center Drive
Los Alamitos, CA 90720
Phone: (800) 241-1771
Web site: www.friedas.com
A WIDE VARIETY OF PRODUCE.

**INDIAN HARVEST
SPECIALTIFOODS**
1012 Paul Bunyon Drive SE
Bemidji, MN 56601
Phone: (800) 346-7032
Web site: www.indianharvest.com
BELUGA LENTILS, QUINOA,
AND MUCH MORE.

**MELISSA'S / WORLD
VARIETY PRODUCE**
P.O. Box 21127
Los Angeles, CA 90021
Phone: (800) 588-0151
Web site: www.melissas.com
FRESH AND DRIED LATIN AMERICAN
PRODUCE, CHILES, GRAINS, AND MORE.

MO HOTTA MO BETTA
P.O. Box 1026
Savannah, GA 31402
Phone: (800) 462-3220
Web site: www.mohotta.com
HOT SAUCES, SPICES, CHILES,
ANNATTO SEEDS, AND MORE.

PENZEYS SPICES
Brookfield, WI
Phone: (800) 741-7787
Fax: (262) 679-7878
Web site: www.penzeys.com
A WIDE VARIETY OF SPICES.

TROPIC-GOOD DISTRIBUTORS
33-60 55th Street
Woodside, NY 11377
Phone: (718) 533-7181
A VARIETY OF LATIN AMERICAN
INGREDIENTS.

WILLIAMS-SONOMA
Phone: (877) 812-6235
Web site: www.williams-sonoma.com
SPICES, IMPORTED PRODUCTS,
KITCHEN EQUIPMENT, AND MORE.

Index

Table of Equivalents

The exact equivalents in the following tables
have been rounded for convenience.

LIQUID/DRY MEASURES

METRIC	U.S.
1.25 milliliters	1/4 teaspoon
2.5 milliliters	1/2 teaspoon
5 milliliters	1 teaspoon
15 milliliters	1 tablespoon (3 teaspoons)
30 milliliters	1 fluid ounce (2 tablespoons)
60 milliliters	1/4 cup
80 milliliters	1/3 cup
120 milliliters	1/2 cup
240 milliliters	1 cup
480 milliliters	1 pint (2 cups)
960 milliliters	1 quart (4 cups, 32 ounces)
3.84 liters	1 gallon (4 quarts)
28 grams	1 ounce (by weight)
454 grams	1 pound
1 kilogram	2.2 pounds

LENGTH

METRIC	U.S.
3 millimeters	1/8 inch
6 millimeters	1/4 inch
12 millimeters	1/2 inch
2.5 centimeters	1 inch

OVEN TEMPERATURE

CELSIUS	FAHRENHEIT	GAS
120	250	1/2
140	275	1
150	300	2
160	325	3
180	350	4
190	375	5
200	400	6
220	425	7
230	450	8
240	475	9
260	500	10